Other giftbooks in this series

Birthday Boy!

Sorry

Little things mean a lot

Go Girl!

I love you madly

Published simultaneously in 2007 by Helen Exley Giftbooks in Great Britain and Helen Exley Giftbooks LLC in the USA.

12 11 10 9 8 7 6 5 4 3 2

Illustrations © Caroline Gardner Publishing and Helen Exley, 2005, 2007
Text, selection and arrangement © Helen Exley 2007
The moral right of the author has been asserted.

ISBN 13: 978-1-84634-089-5

Words by Stuart and Linda Macfarlane
Edited by Helen Exley
Pictures by Roger Greenhough and Caroline Gardner
Printed in China

Helen Exley Giftbooks, 16 Chalk Hill, Watford, Herts WD19 4BG, UK

www.helenexleygiftbooks.com

Birthday Girl!

By Stuart &
Linda Macfarlane

A HELEN EXLEY GIFTBOOK

Good morning!
Happy Birthday!
The moment you have
waited 364 days for
has finally arrived.

Not a second to waste! Get out of bed!

It's your birthday – a day for FUN!

Let there be music and dancing.
Let there be a kaleidoscope
of balloons. Let sweet-scented petals
cascade from the sky.
Today is your birthday.

Shout! Cheer! Jump for joy!
It's your birthday –
a celebration of your life.

Yippeeee, yippeeee, yippeeee, yippeeee,
Yippeeee, yippeeee, yippeeee, yippeeee,
yippeeee, yippeeee, yippeeee, yippeeee,
yippeeee, yippeeee, yippeeee, yippeeee,
yippeeee, yippeeee, yippeeee, yippeeee,
yippeeee, yippeeee, yippeeee, yippeeee,
yippeeee, yippeeee, yippeeee, yippeeee,

It's your birthday!

Birthday girl,
you are a precious gem,
a cause for joy.

You Girl! You are:
Better than the best.
A breath of fresh air.
A shooting star.
An oasis in a desert.
More precious than gold.
More sparkly than diamonds.
You are extra special.
Have a wonderful birthday.

Ring the bell,
Bang the gong,
Beat the drum,
Sound the horn,
It's your birthday.

Put up the bunting –
   raise the flag.
It's your birthday.
A day of celebration
   that will last 365 days!

You should be
completely surrounded by flowers
on your birthday.
Roses to reflect your romantic nature,
tulips for your dreamy side,
and carnations to
complement your loyal personality.
I wish you a
happy birthday bouquet.

Whether eight or eighty,
rich or poor,
schoolgirl or
a great leader,
everyone
loves their birthday.

Fantastic!

Amazing!

Outstanding!

Stupendous

Incredible!

Wonderful!

Superb!

Exciting!

Tremendous!

Spectacular!

Brilliant!

I hope your day will be ALL of these.

Hinting about
    what gifts you want:
Send an email – every ten minutes.
    Have an airplane tow a
        banner across the sky.
    Create the website
        www.what-to-buy-me.com.

ift ideas under doormat

If I could give you
the world for your
birthday, I would.
Wrapped up in rainbows
and glittered with stars.

If I had a wish,
I would give to you;
The brightest star in the sky.
An ocean full of dolphins and whales.
A desert that stretches for
ten thousand miles.
You are such a wonderful person,
nothing in your life
should ever be ordinary.
It should be spectacular.

May your birthday be a day to remember. A day blessed with love, fun and joy.

Today you
must laugh and dance
and sing and only do the
things you really enjoy.

I hope your birthday,
sparkles, shimmers
and goes off
with a bang!

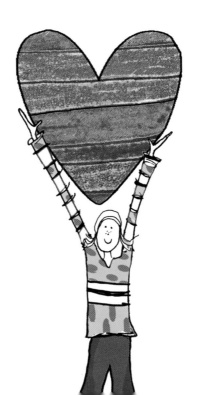

May your birthday
be wrapped
in love,
joy and
happiness.

Make the most of
every moment of this day.
Have the craziest,
happiest time ever.

Birthday:
The one day when it's
definitely better to
receive than to give.

A birthday is
a perfect excuse
for wearing
something really silly.

How to spot a birthday girl:
She's teetering along on
her new Prada shoes,
Wearing smart Versace jeans,
Plugged into the latest MP3,
Texting a friend
And a beaming smile
stretches from ear to ear.

Dance today.
Sing today.
Abandon all care.
Forget all work.
This is a time
for rapturous revelry.

*M*any happy returns
   to you on this special day.
But more importantly,
      may you be blessed
with happiness,
      today and every day.

In the hullabaloo
of your birthday celebrations
take a few moments to
look back on the year
and feel proud of
everything you have done.

A Happy Birthday is...
being with friends.

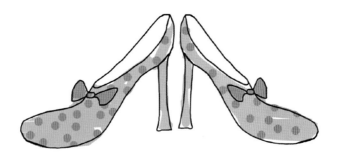

A Happy Birthday is...
using your birthday money
to buy shoes everyone
will disapprove of.

Go wild on your birthday –
gorge yourself with cake and
masses of ice cream.
Leave being sensible till
your next birthday.

W hat I dreamed of getting.

What I got.

A romantic musical.

A "soap" on the TV.

A trip to Disneyland.

A trip to the dentist.

A top-of-the-range iPod.

A donation of a used radio.

An amazing makeover.

Some green nail varnish.

The best present
isn't necessarily something
very expensive –
often a simple gift
given with love and consideration
outshines all the others.

A Happy Birthday is...
being surrounded by love.

May your biggest
and best gift
be lots and lots and lots
of happiness.

The best part of a birthday
is the end of the day when you can stand
quietly and think about all the
wonderful presents you received
and all the fun you had
with your friends.

The party was over.
All the food had been eaten.
All the presents opened.
The weary birthday girl
climbed the stairs.
It had been the best
birthday ever but,
in a funny sort of way,
she was glad it was over –
now she could start
looking forward to her
next birthday.

It's a tragedy!
It's a disaster!
It's a sad, sad fact!
It will not be your birthday,
for another
three-hundred-and-sixty-four days.

May your year be
filled with rainbow days.

May your life be one long,
happy birthday party.

May each day of your life,
Be wrapped up in joy,
happiness and love.

Helen Exley runs her own publishing company
which sells giftbooks in more than seventy countries.
Helen's books cover the many events and emotions in life,
and she was eager to produce a book to say a simple 'sorry'.
Caroline Gardner's delightfully quirky 'elfin' cards
provided the inspiration Helen needed to go ahead
with this idea, and from there this series of stylish
and witty books quickly grew.

Caroline Gardner Publishing has been producing beautifully
designed stationery from offices overlooking the River Thames
in England since 1993 and has been developing the distinctive
'elfin' stationery range over the last five years.
There are also several new illustrations created especially for
these books by artist Roger Greenhough.

Stuart and Linda Macfarlane live in Glasgow, Scotland.
They have produced several books with Helen Exley
including *The Little Book of Stress*, *Old Wrecks' Jokes*,
and the hugely successful *Utterly adorable cats*.